Someone Is Breathing

poems by

J. Morris

DOS MADRES
2018

DOS MADRES PRESS INC.
P.O.Box 294, Loveland, Ohio 45140
www.dosmadres.com   editor@dosmadres.com

Dos Madres is dedicated to the belief that the small press is essential to the vitality of contemporary literature as a carrier of the new voice, as well as the older, sometimes forgotten voices of the past. And in an ever more virtual world, to the creation of fine books pleasing to the eye and hand.

Dos Madres is named in honor of Vera Murphy and Libbie Hughes, the "Dos Madres" whose contributions have made this press possible.

Dos Madres Press, Inc. is an Ohio Not For Profit Corporation and a 501 (c) (3) qualified public charity. Contributions are tax deductible.

Executive Editor: Robert J. Murphy

Illustration & Book Design: Elizabeth H. Murphy
www.illusionstudios.net

Student Intern: Jack Anderson

Typeset in Adobe Garamond Pro & Courier
ISBN978-1-948017-05-3
Library of Congress Control Number: 2018936308

First Edition
Copyright 2018 J. Morris
All rights reserved. No part of this book may be reproduced or transmitted in any form or by any means graphic, electronic or mechanical, including photocopying, recording, taping or by any information storage or retrieval system, without the permission in writing from the publisher.
Published by Dos Madres Press, Inc.

ACKNOWLEDGMENTS

Thank you to the poets, readers, and communities who made these poems better and supported their author, especially Peter Klappert, Robbie Murphy, The Writer's Center, Seekers Church, The Joaquin Miller Cabin Reading Series, the Arlington County (Va.) Department of Parks, Recreation, and Community Resources, and Fishamble (Dublin) Poetry Broadsheets.

Thank you to the editors who liked and published these poems – and who continue against all odds to produce the magazines that keep American poetry alive.

Very special gratitude to Robert Murphy, Elizabeth Murphy, and all at Dos Madres Press.

Most of all, my endless thanks to Katie Fisher for her love, patience, enthusiasm, and spirit.

Grateful acknowledgment is made to the following magazines, in which some of these poems first appeared:

American Arts Quarterly: "What It Loved or Wanted"
Antietam Review: "Trick"
Apalachee Quarterly: "My Skull-Box"
Asheville Poetry Review: "The Form of Loneliness"
Atlanta Review: "The Ropes"
Aura: "The Collection Reviewed"
The Baltimore Review: "Executor"
Brittle Star: "Someone Is Breathing"
The Christian Science Monitor: "Field"
Comstock Review: "Autumn as a Form of Madness"
Cumberland Poetry Review: "Answer to Simmias"
Emrys Journal: "Your Moods Are Orchestral, But"
The Evansville Review: "Perish the Thought,"
    "Civilization and Its Discontents," "Heroics"

The Formalist: "Nabokov's Hundredth Birthday"
Fulcrum: "Selfish Work"
Heliotrope: "The Mark of the Beast"
Illuminations: "Nearly"
Manzanita Quarterly: "Four of a Kind"
Mobius: "The Eighth Rep"
Moving Words: "Don't Ask"
National Poetry Review: "Surface Tension"
Notre Dame Review: "A Sort of Prayer," "The Stupid Club"
Other Poetry: "The Page-Turner"
Pleiades: "This House"
Poet Lore: "Sunset Waltz"
Poetry East: "Fantasy on a Theme by Hallmark," "Only Passing Through"
Poetry International: "Angels," "Reversal"
Prairie Schooner: "The Comforter"
Rock & Sling: "Elvis in Narnia"
Runes: "Brass Danglers"
The Same: "Love Blurbs"
Slant: "The Lodger"
Westview: "Y2K"
West Wind Review: "Johnstown Flood"
Willow Review: "From St. Coletta's," "Divorce"

"The Page-Turner," "The Lodger," "Divorce," "Civilization and Its Discontents," "Field," and "Answer to Simmias" appeared in the chapbook *The Musician, Approaching Sleep* from Dos Madres Press.

TABLE OF CONTENTS

I

My Skull-Box 1
The Lodger 2
A Sort of Prayer 5
Autumn as a Form of Madness 6
The Page-Turner 7
The Form of Loneliness 9
Trick 10
Love Blurbs 11
The Comforter 12
What It Loved or Wanted 14
Indoor Cats 15
Someone Is Breathing 16

II

Brass Danglers 19
Sunset Waltz 20
Divorce 21
Don't Ask 22
Others' Feet 23
Four of a Kind 24
Nabokov's Hundredth Birthday 26
The Mark of the Beast 27
The Stupid Club 28
From St. Coletta's 30
Y2K 31
To Some Citizens of Dixie 32
My Parents' Parties 33
Civilization and Its Discontents 34
Corridor 35
Selfish Work 36
Executor 37

III

Nearly 41
Wake Up 42
Angels 43
Fantasy on a Theme by Hallmark 45
Perish the Thought 46
Reversal 48
The Ropes 49
Surface Tension 50
This House 51
Parables 52
Poem for 2017 59

IV

Field 63
Heroics 64
The Eighth Rep 65
Old School 67
What Being Free Is 68
Answer to Simmias 70
Your Moods Are Orchestral, But 72
The Search Engine Meditates on
    "Guatemala" and "Poetry" 73
Elvis in Narnia 76
The Grave-Digger's Song 77
The Collection Reviewed 79
Only Passing Through 81

About the Author 83

To Katie

I

MY SKULL-BOX

Carved in Indonesia
by a workman who knows his subject,
it rests on the catafalque of my
ink-jet printer.
The little skulls are wide-eyed,
staring round the box-sides
in tragicomic surprise.
On the lid we get the bones –
ribs, exaggerated phalanges –
while inside we get nothing at all
until I choose what to put there.
My wife insisted I keep it in my study,
like a bad pet that can't be trusted.
Okay, jawed and socketed death is not
everyone's favorite companion animal.
There's a puzzle here I've yet to solve:
why the rusted hinge gaping
open is beautiful to me, why
they're so surprised,
why I am not, what to keep
in my skull-box.

THE LODGER

She sensed a figure in the room.
Before the lamp went out, a poem

had inched across her memory,
from early in the century,

when she was young. *I am dreaming.*
The light was gathered in the room

unevenly, a little here,
and there thicker. The comforter

fell from her fingertips, speech
impossible.
            She saw a thatch

of grizzled hair above his parts,
as the light moved with him in the dark,

she saw his chin, bare knobby chest,
belly. *My lodger's mad.* Her sense

of what was light and what was dark
abandoned her. Now she could talk.

She said his name.
                They were both eighty.
Daily greetings, rent paid

the month's first morning, in cash.
A that's-done nod from his neat mustache,

and he took himself back down the hall
and shut his door. Their mutual

respect for privacy was not petty
or rigid. She didn't mind the Verdi

operas he liked to play,
always the same ones, identically

scratched and pocked, and his lips pressed
tight – *I could say much!* – as he kibitzed

from East to North to West to Dummy,
circling her weekly foursome.

    She said his name, but he only took
a small step closer – the floor spoke –

changing what was light and what
was not. *Was not. My lodger's mad*,

his lips pale, yet so imploring,
as if, by taking off his clothing

and crossing the hall and letting the light
touch him in wrinkled, pale, private

places, he meant to ask a question.
She felt no fear at all.
                    At breakfast

she served his coffee, offered cream
and asked him how he'd slept. "I dreamed,"

he said, and sipped. Frowning, he stopped.
She watched him place the sloshing cup

back in its saucer, touch the knot of
his dark green tie.
                She called his daughter

and on the first of the following month
she had no lodger. Surely death

would take him soon, out of the Home.
Vivid at night, poem after poem

returned to her. She felt her youth
retrieve itself. Surely death

would send him naked through the air
to haunt her. She started to prepare.

A SORT OF PRAYER

I'm angry and waiting for snow, needing it,
a swirled and suffocating lock
slapped on the house. Confine me,
give me silence, day upon day,
the still imprisonment, no engines,
no work, even the voices of children
who hurl themselves into the drifts
muffled and flat, the baffles of snow
pulling each sound deeper and destroying
echo, resonance, crystal by crystal.
I need to go deeper, hold myself quieter,
pace to and fro in a snow-socked home
as if it were my monastery. Chanting
a liturgy I've never heard before.
Where is your blizzard, Lord, where
is that saving cold fury? I need it
inside me; failing that, cover the sun
and stars with snow-pillows that burst,
blankets, sheets, put the entire world
to bed, and my old life to sleep
like the dog who once was faithful
but now snarls in his blindness.

AUTUMN AS A FORM OF MADNESS

That sound . . . Acorn dropped,
struck and stopped dead.

And the leaves have lost control,
tossed from their calm green order,
crying yellow and scarlet,
then shuddering, leaping, wet
with melted rime.
Small grass-lives just can't go on:
they wither without protest and choke.
Poplars hear voices, freeze.
The wind grins and forces branches
to scratch the moon's face:
these limbs need restraint.
Soon enough the drug of snow will settle
root- and dirt-nerves. Wise talk –
Thanksgiving, Christmas – may intend
a cure. But only time does any good,
time does all the good it can. Listen:

the infinitely sane
buzz of bees.

THE PAGE-TURNER

is understood to be invisible,

perched beyond the lowest octave,
poised, a tense handmaiden, eyes
faithful to the score, ready to release
the hands clenched

prayerfully in her lap. Pizzicato
cello-strings quiver. Violin-
and viola-bows leap up, a trio of shuttles
warp-weaving,

the pianist's fingers threading the weft.
Now the notes are running out of room,
she leans, then she thrusts
a bare arm out

into the loom's fabric, her fingers
seize the recto corner and freeze.
Perilous moment! We are not meant to notice
her, the rapt gaze

fastened on her maestro's face,
waiting for that cue, impersonal –
curt nod, lofted eyebrow, even a deeper
breath – that gives

permission to the page-turner, that says
Now I need you!, and she performs
so swiftly, all elegance and clarity
in the turning,

accomplished. Then tacet once more,
waiting, returned beyond the lowest
possibility of sound, to listen,
to watch. As we watch

what is woven yet can't be seen,
the beauty calling the quintet
and us to gather – all unseen.
We go home,

make our customary mistakes, confuse
visible signs with invisible grace.
But as sleep deranges us, perhaps
we hear the tapestry

and glimpse a silent turning of the page.

THE FORM OF LONELINESS

He killed a hornet, became catastrophe
with looming, swift, left Nike.
Shining forms burst in the cattails, and hunger

drove him away. He drove to a cafeteria,
filled his tray with meats and cakes.
A learned Greek could grasp his culture entire.

Greeks: it made him remember pornography.
Scum spat out from slick stalks.
The woman's anus wet like an open sore.

Angles, trapezoids, parabolas:
he'd watched the wind-made water-shapes
go flying down the surface of the pond,

wind-thoughts giving birth to geometry.
Perhaps it started so, with the Greeks.
Philosophy begins in wonder.

TRICK

In dreams a dead friend is sly,
unwilling to say precisely how
or why he fooled you, fooled his daughters, his wife.
But knowledge curls in his smile

(which isn't quite right, which isn't the smile
he had before he did the trick)
and suggests a reason, several reasons,
you would approve if you could go

without sleeping. Till then,
trust the reappearance. He and the wet earth
had a misunderstanding. You were weeping,
you blinked and missed – there at the grave-

side – how they embraced and started over.
In dreams your sly friend is alive
but smiling, saying *I can explain*,
but only and ever smiling.

LOVE BLURBS

Fascinating, brilliant, beautiful – unlike anything I've ever seen before.

I was up all night with this one.

Uncompromising yet charming, her style is irresistible.

I couldn't put her down.

Can't wait to see more of her work.

*

A new tone of realism – at times grim, but always frank – pervades her latest.

The mature commitment to character and complex themes is unsettling and powerful.

Flashes of . . . wit and . . . insight enliven this stark family chronicle.

A demanding tale, full of the drama and conflict we've come to expect from [her].

*

Disappointing.

The protagonists are hard to admire, or even like.

Her promising debut is only recalled in certain phrases and poignant details.

I was prepared to love this one, but had trouble finishing it. And I was glad when it was over.

THE COMFORTER

His voice so calm and rational,
appreciative, brandy-smooth.
Not terribly snobbish in his
pronunciation of *Le sacre du printemps*,
but making a good-faith effort
to deliver a Gallic nasality
on the first syllable of spring.
I welcome this baritone spirit
into my little living room,
for the city surrounds me,
which certainly means I am afraid.
He will give me something Baroque
next, he assures me. In the kitchen
my wife runs water loudly, like static.
I want that assurance, I want comfort,
I want to keep out the jamming pulse
of my angry polytonal nation,
and I want to keep my wife.
Both desires are lately in question.
He smiles from the speakers
and, in describing a Telemann concerto,
seems to bless a community of the wavebands,
a united state of good music lovers.
The union will forever be exclusive.
At this moment I can't see
why it's so wrong to want that.
I even think that God might speak so:
rich tones, full of culture,
inviting us all to Heaven,
securing us against intruders,
conversant in European languages
but refusing a too precious purse
of the lips. The umlauted *schön*

he leaves a touch imperfect,
in honor of Babel, but then pours his love
and protection down through the cellos,
and fifty thousand watts, and wires.

WHAT IT LOVED OR WANTED

At dusk my UV lamp stained
lilac the white towel nailed
beneath it to the porch rail.
Out of the nervous mutter of almost-rain,
a Polyphemus came to the light:
huge, one Cyclops eye blinking
with every beat of each back wing.
My camera blinded him, then restored his sight

in sequence, flash after flash. Benign
equipment compared to my childhood net,
jar, poison, pin: death
proving, I think, beauty: hard, though, to re-mind
that childhood self, remember what
it loved or wanted. In your absence,
in silence, I placed
on the table beside the moth – eyespots

staring, gone stiff and frightened –
your photograph, the one I trimmed
to fit my wallet. Your image eyed him,
I measured both of you, focused, found
a frame that seemed to work, and took
the shot. Proving, I think, something
about size, the comparison – *this thing
was bigger than a wallet-photo, look!* –

you had no interpretation
to offer, being nowhere near,
and the rain tore,
drop by drop, a hole in the composition.

INDOOR CATS

Like indoor cats we're curious and scared
to get on the wrong side
of the front door. We stare out the window
and don't know the names. We remember
those times we were transported

into that bright windy world:
doors slammed, motors gunned,
and at journey's end
someone hurt us for our own good
as we hissed and writhed.

Now and then the door swings open.
We know we could squeeze through.
We give the porch a bitter glance,
then make a fuss, asking for kibble and
a lap.

SOMEONE IS BREATHING

Get a fresh disease and it's like an immersion
language course – you plunge into the generic names,
the regimens and prognoses. You learn a new patter.

I staggered into the ER. *Something,*
I croaked as they gang-bundled me
into the wheelchair, *in the air, I seem to be allergic,*
the words staggering too, mixed up with rapid wheezes

and wretched snoring gasps, the background sound
of mere breathing now a hoarse roar.
Back at home, back to normal, I sit here meaning to listen
to a Brahms string quartet but not paying much attention,

preoccupied with the muttered babbling-on
of these foreign voices; I'm trying to figure out
when the Intal inhaler I ordered from Canada might arrive;
it's a leukotriene receptor antagonist . . . and then I hear it.

We're in the slow movement, the cello gruff and soft,
gentle twangs from pizzicato violins. Someone is breathing.
Where is it, in the stereo pan? Toward the right . . . the viola?
Yes, again: the tiniest indrawn nasal hiss,

just before the minor third is plucked.
Shouldn't the engineer have caught that, called for a retake?
No. It's human, imperfect, it's someone really sitting there,
playing for dear life, and I'm sure the poor man

is breathing as quietly as he can.

II

BRASS DANGLERS

Your dad's got balls, I'll tell you.
We wheeled him in here not knowing
what the hell was wrong, and he's
joking, kind of apologizing, acting
like it's no big deal. Talk about
brass danglers.

I had occasion, a little later, to see
the balls themselves. Small, hidden,
and the penis delicate in its
fluffy nest of old white down.
My father was nearly screaming by then:
with a fair degree of clinical interest,
a different doctor'd injected him with a quick-
acting antidote to morphine – the same
shot used to revive the blue-mouthed junkie –
and all tolerance for pain, all guts, had
vanished. Everything hurt, all at once, and
badly, and he'd crapped himself, so he lay naked
on the ER gurney, with me gripping his shoulder
and trying not to look,
looking elsewhere for the lost dignity –
unable to find it, of course, lost is lost –
while his face contorted and he gave answers,
between groans and pleas, that proved,
to all our satisfaction, the return
of his customary lucidity, now that the overdose
was undercut. So it wasn't a stroke. So
he'll be fine. Just took one too many pain
pills accidentally.

Yes, I told the doctor,
I'm next of kin. I'll inherit everything.
I came from there: child of the Brass Danglers,
and of the thin, sparsely thatched tool.

SUNSET WALTZ

My mother has lost almost all of the lovable
bits of herself by now: the gaiety goes,
self-pity survives, and confusion, and terrible
trouble untangling the quick from the dead. Anger at those
who conspire against her – my father, her niece – delusion,
resistance, confusion – did I say that already? Dementia
is catching, I find myself losing
the thread of my thoughts and intentions,
repeating the same few must-do items
on lists that I write and rewrite.
Jewelry. Cigarettes. Power of attorney?
I'm kind. I'm certain.
I'm stern. I act like I know
what I'm doing. And finally it's done,
we're ready to go,
Mom can be moved into Sunset –
no, really, it's Sunrise, but who are they kidding?
The sun won't rise in a lucid sky for her anymore.
I rise to the challenge, I manage to keep the conspiracy hidden
and get her the hell out the door,
I set her down gently, the nurses will guard her
in rooms bright and tiny, with 24-hour assistance.
When I say *We love you* (saying *I love you* is harder)
her eyes become blurry, the fears and suspicions
forgotten along with her age and the name
of her husband – *I know you do*,
she always responds, baffled but game,
willing to somehow believe it – *And I love you too*
– at least for a moment, and then
she goes crazy again.

DIVORCE

They made the vow at City Hall, Manhattan,
June, 'forty-six. Ring, license. The JP
invoked obedience, honor, fidelity
"till death do you part." *I do.* And that was that,
and no one there to cry. The bridegroom lied;
he never meant to honor her. She never
did obey him. They staggered on, tethered
for fifty-four sad, ragged years, and died

eight weeks apart. *They're with each other now
forever,* says the priest. The JP spoke
a kinder truth, I think. The earthly blunder
stopped with Heaven. Death revoked the vow
my parents never kept and never broke.
Let none re-yoke what God has pulled asunder.

DON'T ASK

We *raised the question* and first it hovered vaguely
like a spook at a seance, and then we raised it again
even higher until we both had to salute it.
So we thought we'd better *table the question*
but it rattled the plates and cutlery and would not
take polish. What left but to *call the question?*
Here it came, romping like a puppy gone goofy over
its own name. We couldn't get rid of it.
No, we said, *bad* question, we don't want you,
but we answered it anyway, and now I live alone.

OTHERS' FEET

Insects dance on three pairs of legs, and tap six feet
(tarsi, properly, tipped by claws), while the trope for "grave"
dates to the Great Plague, Pepys, Defoe: dead meat,
the Lord Mayor decreed, corrupts the living; he gave
the rule, and the figure: *six feet under*. Yet to compete
with other men (my father figured) you had to brave
the heights in the other direction: *You hit six feet!*
my small Pop crowed when, surly, prickly, needing to shave,
at fourteen and change I cowered beneath his pencil.
                                                          Arrange

six musical feet. Hemiola: arrange the beats
into three groups of two, two groups of three. It's strange
but true: the stress creates space, the dance defeats
time. My foolish Muse, why then must I divide
the oldest concord of all, and, counting, choose a side?

FOUR OF A KIND

Guts Poker

Six fists thrust out over a rich pot.
I've got a sweaty chip clutched
in mine. When the fingers spring open,
I could rake it all in. I can see it:
mine the only chip to drop, all the other men
admiring my Guts.
In fact, two other men
have Guts. My flush is a loser, I match the pot,
the pot is now twice as rich, I am half as rich,
and Guts goes on, Guts never stops until five men
empty (No Guts. No Guts. No Guts. No Guts. No Guts.
Guts.) their fists.

Low-Ball Poker

I'm trying to have
the worst hand. Ordinari-
ly this is easy.

      *

Western Zen: The worst
hand is the best hand. Dealer's
choice. Deuce. Satori.

      *

I need a seven.
Give it to me now, o deck
shuffled long ago.

      *

What was the color of your ace before the King and Queen were born?

      *

What is the sound of one hand folding?

Follow the Queen

She's wild. She turns up
and the following card
goes wild as well. And wild in my hand.
Regal, fickle: the next time she's dealt,
she removes wildness and bestows it
on a different card. And should she come last,
the last to be revealed,
then only the Lady is wild,
the Lady is anything
(and it's only a game) I want her to be.

Woofer's Revenge

The first choice is free: do I want it? Which way am I going?
I'll see the second choice: it costs a buck. I could
go high or low. No, let's look at the third choice,
which costs two bucks. And the last choice is
no choice at all, three bucks required, like it or not.
My hole cards aren't speaking to me. I should
fold, let Woofer have his revenge.
I've never met Woofer but, on the evidence,
he is some kind of existentialist
with a grudge, dealing me choice
after choice: Jean-Paul Woofer.
I should have taken the freebie.

NABOKOV'S HUNDREDTH BIRTHDAY

"What's left to give a happy genius?"
— *Pierre Delalande*

Dear Sir: I did not think I needed
an Apple full of bytes and RAM
(my memory has far exceeded
the formatting of who I am),
but once I "booted up" — if that is
the proper term? — and checked the status
of various "browsers," began to race
my mouse through mazes of hyper-space —
this centenarian was enchanted!
A world-wide web of hyper-sense . . .
a pedant's perfect present tense . . .
the linked scholia I always wanted . . .
I thank you, Sir! best wishes from
<VN@lol.com>.

Vladimir Nabokov celebrated his hundredth birthday on April 23, 1999, quietly, in Montreux, Switzerland, with his wife and son and a few friends.

THE MARK OF THE BEAST

The day is done, my dear – you're looking smart
in Hot-Sleep Sox and PJs by CG,
a name and logo stitched across the heart

and on each ankle. Jeans and tops cry "Bart"
and "Hilfiger": tomorrow's panoply.
The day is done, my dear. You're looking smart

but acting dumb, dear one. Why did you start
this loathsome bout of free publicity,
a name and logo stitched across the heart

of each display of crass designer-art?
You used to wear a cross. Obviously
that day is done. My "Dear, you're looking smart"

is daily less sincere. And I can chart
the likely course of this idolatry,
a name and logo stitched across the heart

of everything you are. When you depart
for warmer climes, your master will agree:
"Your day is done, my dear – you're looking smart,
my name and logo stitched across your heart."

THE STUPID CLUB

Such clear eyes and careful speech.
He owned a video rental club in Duck,
North Carolina, enjoyed real death captured
on tape:

and it was astonishing how often
this happened: the Super-8 at hand to be set whirring
while your friend is eviscerated by a bear: historic records
of garrotings

filmed by patriots: and of course
the classic exploding head, found art, *de M. Zapruder.*
His taste was bad enough, but I resented his attempts
to rent me

his favorites — an oenophile
praising vintages. *Did* I want to see them?
Four years later, Kurt Cobain has . . . what is the term
policemen use?

Sucked death? Eaten lead? Young man with
a gun, an infant daughter, fame, money,
talent, a mother, a heroin addiction, fans
who loved him,

loved ones who didn't. Hmmmm. From this
list he selected the gun. His mother says
he often spoke of suicide. *I told him*, she says,
not to join

that stupid club. Membership in
the Stupid Club is often a big letdown
to the elected. Show us the note he left and let us
learn

what he expected. With all his wealth,
surely he bought a camcorder along the way.
Why be old-fashioned? Turn the thing on, secure it on
the tripod,

point it at your chair, walk over
and take your place. Talk. Goodbyes: sloppy
slurring fucked-head articulation. He makes a point
of telling

whomever it may concern, *Sell it,
I want you to, let any fan see it who wants to.*
Old red-eye winks at him. He makes eye contact, raises
the shotgun,

fits the twin barrels between
tongue and palate. The taste makes him gag.
Hurry up. An instant classic for my man
in Duck.

FROM ST. COLETTA'S

From St. Coletta's came all the special ones,
Halloween guests at our nonprofit office.
Escorted by the school staff, masked or daubed
in clown paint, they whooped and stumbled, and those who could
demanded *Trick or treat!* and those who could
held out their bags. I gave them treats
because, for ten minutes, they were there,
not because I feared a retaliatory trick.
They were in no shape to egg my car
or burn a bag of shit on my doorstep.
Stunned Raggedy Ann in your red wig and wheelchair,
here is a Milky Way. Silent grinning Zorro, here is
a Snickers, just for you. Happy
Halloween, it's my treat, my pleasure, it's
the least I can do. It's the most I can do.
Not everyone is called to walk beside you
and curl your fingers round the sweets,
not everyone, but a few:

the teachers of St. Coletta's.
I told them *Thanks for coming* and *Good
to meet you*, wincing in the glare of their love.
I said *Goodbye*. I went back
to my cubicle, limping, blinking,
back to work, plucking at the painful taut
elastic band around my head, and
I am not special at all, am I?

Y2K

Home in bed at midnight and no,
my electric clock did not blink out
and yes, my megawatted reading bulb
burned on, illuminating the first
complete sentence of the current thousand years,
and all was Y2K-compliant.
The Western world pays for the best
and gets it.

Below, in the road, the usual cracks
and booms and hoots as revelers
tossed their expensive jollity into space.
Then, rolling into the room, came a thunder.
It grumbled like the other side of the planet,
powerful, unavoidable, and densely
populated. Came and went, and my light held steady,
and a whizbang swooped past the window,
burst into two. For the moments that
I rolled with it, I almost thought
The kooks were right . . . Ridiculous
to say I was frightened,
just briefly. I give the scare to you:
an appointment to take with us
onto the empty calendar,
as the triple-zero payoff rings the bell, our machine
loaded, not with cash,
but with a millennium of mounting, awful debt.

This poem was written in 2000, before the Towers fell.

TO SOME CITIZENS OF DIXIE

It's easy enough to mind your manners
and easier still to simply act the part.
It's hard to mend a century's damage,
and harder still to rip your icy heart
out, to let it melt for a Black batter
as you stand, hatless, squinting in the glare,
gamely mouthing "The Star-Spangled Banner"
beneath the waving Stars and Bars' red stare.

You shrug and call them names of their own preference –
African-American? Well, why not?
Bide your time. Conceal your rebel snigger.
Show your charm, your class and deference.
A mere name can fire the first shot;
a single rhyme, uttered, pulls the trigger.

MY PARENTS' PARTIES

The Negro cop was sober – the only one present
who was, I expect – and fingered the pellet-pocks –
"Air gun, mam" – and said he'd ask his lieutenant
to check on local hoods, creeps, punks.
My parents' party sizzled with speculation
(invasion seemed to threaten us that spring):
delinquents popping windows, or revolution?
"The *blacks*," said one fine guest. "He should 'ax' that King."

King got his, more windows needed fixing,
but no one smashed the "Welcome to Maryland" sign,
no armies marched across the D.C. line
to crash my parents' parties. Riots, singing:
crap. We all relaxed and elected Nixon.
Pellets aren't bullets. Just ax that King.

CIVILIZATION AND ITS DISCONTENTS

The infant's desires are, in compass, small
(milk, a soothing hand, clean Pampers) and carry
no threat to comity. Older children also
are limited in what they might demand –
undeveloped imaginations, too shallow
dredgings of *want* and *need*. No reason not to
free them, more or less, let them enjoy
their tantrums, give them toys, weave stories at bedtime.
(We do well, though, to keep the kittens
safe from their experimental sticks and thumbs.)
But soon, far too soon, a terrible grief:
the capacity for desiring bloats and explodes,
its possible satisfactions multiply,
touch the unknowable, and know neither order
nor decency. Can we picture the full indulgence
of any man's wants, any woman's? All moral fetters
removed, the world lined up and organized
to truly please? Shades of de Sade, of Dachau.
It is so sad, that we are so wrong in ourselves
that stern renunciation becomes both right and
the only practical way to get along.
Shouldn't we, then, pamper the babes, serve them,
rush to respond to each whimpered velleity?
They'll have to stop that nonsense soon enough –
at least allow them the memory of perfect pleasure.
Or would that only make their lives sadder?

CORRIDOR

In the hospital corridor I smell something
I don't like – a sharp scientific tang,
full of isotopes and control – beneath it
sour body-stuff, wastes, sweats.
It puts me off my food. It scares me to death.
I think of my cat, who's eighteen and deaf
and, recently, blind: she gets by on smells,
her nose an outthrust, anxious sentinel
as she bumps among the once-familiar furniture.
Stiff-legged, punch-drunk, howling, confounded by corners,
she makes it to her bowl of reeky fish.
Hard to imagine her loving such a stench,
hard to believe the stench is all she has.
The corridor turns – Room 10 – "It's you," he says.

SELFISH WORK

Not everyone gets the death he deserves –
I can imagine Mark stricken
far from home, his screams
echoing out of *l'hôpital,*
and *les médecins* wondering who to call –

but it did happen close by, and slowly
enough. His brother slept in the chair,
or didn't sleep. His friends
present to the touch. A circle firm
as flesh can make it: *that* is earned,

such a man has given friendship
down the years, gripped hands,
given again. But not now.
Dying is selfish work. And whose life
do I grip, Mark? If

I start to cough blood, if my flesh withers
or, crossing Independence, a truck
knocks me into the countdown,
who will gather, and for how long?
When I scream, *Tell me how soon!*

who will answer? No siblings or children
or lover. Friends, then. I'm afraid
I've cherished too selfishly.
The work is more than half-begun.
What I deserve is the question.

EXECUTOR

You gave me, between gasps, instructions
for several of your stories: an episode
we both agreed should probably come out,
a character you felt had wandered in
like a *right talky* Danville neighbor,
visiting from a nearby story
remembered but as yet not written down.
You gave me the file names, and thanked me – you who thanked
every nurse and orderly, every baffled friend.
I'm calling you up now, several times a week.
You're virtually real, nearly available, conjured
amidst the codes. Visiting. I wish we could consult,
I wish I had your permission to make this rather longer cut,
to stitch these scenes together – here – and here –
you *do* see that it works?
And if I have you at my fingertips, why,
it's like having you back: here is your voice,
assured, delicate, whimsical: but chary of reply.

III

NEARLY

It ought to have a name, the look
we feel compelled to send back
to treacherous turf, the bad curb
that trips us up and nearly sends us sprawling.
Balance regained, self righted,
we take our cue. Frowning, thoughtful,
our face a face for all the world
to see (it says *I'm seeking information,*
I'm willing to know why I failed,
why the step-by-step skills
I learned before I learned my name
have let me down. See me pay attention!),
we stop, glance, ponder, and prove
the lesson of that shameful stumble
isn't lost on us – we never
play the fool by striding off as if

a near-disaster doesn't matter.

WAKE UP

Like snow – both flake and fall – my self
comes down to sleep, taking shapes
from the ground that waits below.
Mutilations. A slow ragged
severing of my testicles
with cold water and blows
hurled into my face to keep me conscious.
First the right, then the left
eyeball sucked from the socket
(my head clamped in a vise)
until each dangles from its strong
optic nerve, then the strings are wrapped
around two fingers and wetly plucked
from my brain.
                Forgive me, my love,
for telling you. Forgive me, but
you lie beside me in the dark.
Here in the borderland, disassembled,
accumulating, my body
has fallen into the torturer's hands,
and I can descend no further. Two friends
died last year, conformed themselves
to the waiting ground. Forgive me
if I writhe and kick and hiss breath
into my lungs, and force myself to try
to cross the only other border,
clutching your hand and whispering,
Wake up.

ANGELS

Cold, cold, cold,

frigid, trapped Christmas: his friends
have sent him cards with angels on them.
They haunt the window ledge, golden.

Outside, ice imprisons the streets.
I see the clear delineation
between what's frozen and what escapes:
no slight wet border, no thawing by day.
It fell as ice, as ice it lies
in smooth, dangerous shapes.

From the hospital window he saw angels.
They seemed to glory in single digits,
broken sun, bad tidings.
They were out in record numbers.
Drugs for the dying: he saw angels
dancing on the air outside.

Lights on in the opposite wing,
snowfall blown against gravity:
the consubstantiation of angels.
How they're formed, like art: it's all
in how we see, and then the declaring.
All different, nothing changed.

Christmas angels holding trumpets,
face-front in their cardboard ranks.
Are they like these? I want to know.
He can't speak, but shakes his head,
his fingers flutter, gesture: *plenitude,
lovelier.* Saying *let me go.*

I look out the window too,
and hear his mother whisper the answer
to each mittened and hushed-voiced visitor:

Bad, bad, bad.

FANTASY ON A THEME BY HALLMARK

Some are hallowed and familiar:
Birthday, Happy anniversary,
and *Sympathy*, the one we all will need.
But recently the colored cardboard placards
placed to segregate the neighborhoods,
each ethnic group of greeting cards
descending in rows from its descriptor –
recently these signposts have taken
to marking curious new developments
of sensibility. The cards themselves
suck, of course, and so
I offered a stoned clerk twenty dollars
and now I send the cardboard signs instead.
Cope is useful; a stern imperative.
And *Suitable for remarriage* has
a tart ambiguity: her or me?
Money holder, mailed without comment,
speaks its reproof to mean acquaintances.
Best of all, the series I have lived
so many times and never known how
to subdivide and signify. Now I send *More
than friends,* then *New love*
(*humor*) (God, I guess, is laughing),
then *Troubled love,* then *Sorry.*
A final, noble, sweet effort,
Across the miles, and then the truth:
Blank inside.

PERISH THE THOUGHT

My books are discontent. I can tell:
they crouch, glum, on the tenement shelves.
Some lament their cracked spines,
their tattered faded jackets.
Long novels by female authors
are feeling fat. The latest macho sensation
blushes behind the blurbs gaudy as
unearned medals. A snobby tome
of metaphysics is slashed to
remainders on its rickety table
of contents. Has someone judged them
by their covers, their acid-free innards,
their deckled tummies and dyed flat-tops?

No, much worse than that: a life sentence
to make sense, to keep the world sane:
impossible and they know it, my poor books,
they puff dust and lean left, lean right,
cardboard shacks longing for collapse.
The ruin of my library would be
their liberation. No longer to give their word!
To speak volumes! O to be returned
to pulp and bulk, to illegible atoms!

I won't let them do it, of course.
All slaves have bad days – the master's mood
can be contagious – and mine
will get over this one. Tomorrow,
next week, they'll marshal phonemes,
phrases, tropes, and sing their signifiers
once again. No more questions (how

a pattern of shaped ink talks,
how it says the same thing, first
or *n*th edition, how
we hear it, why we think
this is not madness too) for now.

REVERSAL

The rugs have had too much to drink,
especially that red runner in the hall,
which has always been a little sarcastic
anyway, and now it's playing
stupid practical jokes – I nearly landed on my butt.
The curtains are tipsy too, fluttering and muttering
stuff a boy shouldn't hear.
The ceiling fan is high, the dishwasher's loaded –
look out, here comes a dirty saucepan,
right at my head. Cabinets nipping
from bagged bottles, unmade beds sprawled
unconscious, wobbly chairs bending over backwards,
lamps that brighten, darken, flicker and pop
as the juice flows . . .
Our whole apartment has gone on a binge, and not
for the first time. This place has got a *problem,*
the day will come when all five rooms
cram themselves into some church basement:
Hi, my name is Apartment 912 and I'm an alcoholic.

But moored in the middle like small boats straining
against tautened ropes, my parents
smile at each other, at me, and take my hand.
The square footage is a rhomboid wreck, drunk as a skunk,
but Mom and Pop are sober. Their faces
are orderly and bright, like bills paid on time
and placed each month in a brown accordion file.
That's the way to run a face, to maintain a person –
pay your bills on time. And let the apartment
do what it likes, it's just a bunch of wood and
metal and fabric. You're flesh and spirit.
Stay sober, stay calm, let the walls and whitewash
do the drinking. We're family.

THE ROPES

The grave, as final forwarding address,
holds no terrors for me, really –
it's moving there that chills the failing blood.
I don't mean illness, and giving yourself up
to the dubious mercies of nurses and doctors
(though yes, that's a grisly rendezvous to keep),
but the moment of crossing over,
the side-step or full plunge, the trance or faint
and there you are.
I want someone to show me the ropes of Death.
I'm a newbie, I have no clue
what to do here, what might lie in wait
to hurt me. A fate worse than Death? Don't laugh.
Coming out of the previous void . . . no, I can't remember.
All my earliest memories teem with helpers,
guides, big loving people.
No one made me fledge till I was ready.
Something like that again, please, that's what I want,
a talkative Charon, a smiling Virgil – I'm not particular,
it needn't be a top-tier angel, just a soul
who cares and who's been dead longer.

SURFACE TENSION

The sleek duck holds himself
primped and sculpted on the pond
while below, like galley slaves,
vigorous orange paddles
power the visible animal.

Imagine a brain floating
in the illusion of self-sameness,
unable to feel the work being
done beneath the waterline
of being, famously unable
to sense a cancerous rebellion
of slave-cells. Some insignificant
creatures, it's true, travel
light, on surface tension alone:
the water-strider, a mere bug,
cruises over the molecules
on six dimples, and never crashes
through, its bug-worthy destination
chosen for it by chance propulsion
and simple breezes.

The natural order
may not hold the proper model.
Instead, take a thing made
in our own image: the television,
its penetrable screen sifting
only dust and the odd reflection.
I see through that. I discover
consciousness, violence, laughter,
apparent stories. The repairman,
though (should I ever need him),
ponders a thousand metal and plastic
parts, charged, hot, working,
or not.

THIS HOUSE

This house remembers the day.
Come midnight, it broods still
upon noon. Tomorrow it will
worry yesterday.
Something prowls
from room to room, fires
neuron after neuron, never tires
of holding, mulling. This house scowls

and sighs. And grows
a halo of fireflies,
its thick oak tongue
locked for now, silenced,
hawkmoths and midges flung
like insults against its brows.

PARABLES

i.
Consider the terrorist, who hides
in the rusting blue dumpster
behind the funeral parlor.
His plan is to blow up the building
in the middle of the first service.
All night he has lurked
in the foul-smelling dumpster,
his explosive device strapped
painfully to his torso.
In the early morning,
when the custodial staff open
the rear doors to bring out the trash,
the terrorist will come in.

Don't be like the foolish terrorist!
For he has no need to conceal himself
through the night. He could arrive promptly
in the morning and gain entrance,
smelling of fresh soap. Even as you strive
for complication and subterfuge
in your foul devices, in the same measure
will your parent in heaven reveal
the simplicity of her ways,
at the end of time.
If you can hear this, that's great!

ii.
Once there was a wise copyeditor
who controlled a hundred blue pencils
and these were his joy.
His manager came to him and said,
"I'm going to replace all these pencils

with software and you can take a
longer 'lunch hour.'" The copyeditor
gave away the blue pencils, turned off his lamps
and awaited the installation of the software.
But then the manager came again and said,
"My masters need beautiful writing after all,
and so I must rely on you, my excellent editor."
The two men turned on the lamps,
looked around the office,
and every pencil was gone.
This copyeditor knew all the parts of speech,
he was able to correct the finest points
of grammar and style. But
the promise of obedience blinded him
to his own value, he gave away
that which was most precious to him
and now he is far from the kingdom of heaven.

iii.
The kingdom of heaven is like the rooftop
of a building scheduled for demolition.
Our heavenly parent gathers us there,
calling us to come up carefully
on the crumbling staircases, and to forgive
the ones who would destroy the ancient edifice.
Soon the building will tremble beneath our feet
as the wrecking balls commence their work
and many who themselves tremble will stand fast,
and many who do not feel the tremor will collapse.
Or again, the kingdom of heaven is like a blue elephant.
Nowhere in creation has the king
placed such a beast. It lives imaginatively
if at all. And yet – and this is surely true –
many who conceive of the blue elephant

will come to possess him, and many who scoff
will find themselves trampled beneath his feet
and they will say, "Father, we did not know
you were real! Mother, have mercy on us!"
And our heavenly parents will indeed forgive us,
not once, not seven times, but seventy times seven!

iv.
A bass player bought new strings
for her Ibanez, replacing the old strings
that had grown dirty over the years
she had played them. Proudly she
displayed her newly restrung bass
at the next rehearsal of her band,
but the first guitar player said,
"Those strings are too shiny!"
and the second guitar player said,
"Will they stay in tune, sister?"
And the singer said to her,
"I'm worried those strings may have
been too expensive." And the drummer
said not a word but sadly re-tuned
his floor tom.

Would you have this bass player
hang her head in shame,
after trying only to do what is right?
Then you will not enter the kingdom of heaven.
Blessed is the musician
who strives after righteousness
and remains in the band though
she may hear untrusting words. This player
will make many recordings,
and like the harps of old,
her Ibanez will cry out to the people,
"Praise your heavenly parent!"

v.
A rabbi walks into a bar.

vi.
Once there were ten excellent math teachers.
Each teacher had received awards
commensurate with his or her achievements,
and each was a proud teacher.
"Here are the properties of a triangle!"
one might say, and "I'll show you
how to solve for X!" said another.
The ten excellent math teachers were faultless
in their observances. Now one day a tyrant
took over the school system
and all ten teachers were thrown into prison.
Though they begged and filed grievances and
pointed to their achievements and awards,
the tyrant was unmoved. "Triangles?" he scoffed.
"What use have I for a triangle?" And,
"I don't care what values X may have."

So you see that the excellence of the ten
could not save them from the darkness.
Nor could the school system withstand
tyranny and disdain for mathematics –
it's true, within one year that school system
fell into ruins. So don't be like the math teachers,
mistaking the things they loved best
for the proofs they would need
in a dark season.

vii.
To what can I compare this generation?
We're like poor people who give names
to the fragments and ragged scraps

that constitute our possessions,
saying, "I'd like you to meet Rachel,
my red trashbag tie" and
"Here is my used Band-Aid, Joel."
We are like prisoners who talk to rats
as if they were our good friends.
We plant nothing, we reap nothing,
our translations are so approximate
as to be meaningless in the eyes of the Lord.
But the day is coming when judgment
will at last be withheld, and light
will burst upon us like a thousand suns,
and the pathetic items we possess
will shine brightly –
yes, even the rats will stare in wonder.
Then this lucky generation will bless the day
they believed themselves so poor.

viii.
A rabbi walks into a bar.
A priest, a rabbi, and a snakehandler walk into a bar.
A visually challenged rabbi walks into a priest.
The snakehandler hits the wall.
The rabbi asks the piano player if she knows God.
All the snakes, sick of being handled, go free.
"God is a concept," sings the piano player,
"by which we measure our pain."
The snakehandler hits the priest, a snake, and a sour note.
"Rabboni!" cries the piano player.
The rabbi regrets that he doesn't see very well.
And yet no voice is more lovely than his,
in the bar, on this night when the prophesies are fulfilled.

THE EIGHTH REP

Struggling with the eighth rep
at forty (piece of cake at twenty-five), I hear
a tenor sax, piano, and traps
killing a tune my parents played in Living Stereo:

big bands for big parties, loud and crass,
reduced to this. The dancers too
have dwindled, "elder citizens" who shuffle past
the weight-room doors as "In The Mood"

echoes through the Community Center. Here I press,
sweating. There they touch palms and waists.
We're spending Halloween together –
here an orange head, severed,

flattened – just a cardboard pumpkin –
and there a skeleton – here something
green and evil and dead, hunched behind the drummer.
Another one behind my head.   Back in summer,

when I joined, the Center swarmed
with kids, shooting pool, throwing hopeless layups.
School started, the Center calmed:
homework called, and a free gym. Their protean shapes –

bunnies, gypsies, plastic-masked Madonnas and Barts –
are missing here tonight. No treats.
Couldn't the Center find a way to divide in parts:
old, medium, young? each

part dancing or pressing or going *Boo!*
in separate rooms? all for one and in the mood?
    Eight will do. The saxman blows
hard, then stops. Where *are* they? No,

too late. I think a trick we played
has frightened the little ghouls away.
Only grownups left, a glad community:
the elder citizens, the skeletons and me.

OLD SCHOOL

The thrift-store clerk shuffles over,
slaps the boombox. Moments later,
Old School basslines roil the room.
He's moving off, a spring in his stagger,
eyeing the handful of customers:
Are we getting this? He nods and smiles,
modeling *Yes*, the kid he was
peeking out from behind the mustache, just knowing
we like Barry White.

Nowadays everyone's got their own
private soundtrack rattling in their earbuds.
Do sophomores still celebrate
the perfection of spring by yanking up
the dorm windows, hoisting their speakers
onto the sill, then returning
to the stereo, the volume knob,
and blaring the best music
in the world, at the moment,
out onto the heads of helpless passersby? I hope so.
I doubt it. Stereo. See note.

Autotuned cash-pop in the supermarket
isn't the same. The assistant managers
who make me hear it don't love it,
don't care what it makes me feel.
For God's sake, mean it!
Be Old School, turn it up!
Share your favorite song with me
like a DJ in a thrift store,
the way my neighbor's baby
crawls across the floor
and hands me a sodden pretzel,
drooling a little, certain of my thanks.

WHAT BEING FREE IS

To be or not to be: is that a question?
Philosophers! Unbearable, unless,
like Hamlet, you embody your own puzzle.
The Prince's problem seems both fair and clear.
Nay, it is. I know not seems. But look:
self-slaughter – any other death besides
the one that crowns Act V – can never happen.
Every new performance of Act III
must end with Hamlet on his feet, must send
the Prince to England, *or confine him where
your wisdom best shall think.* From stage to stage
he never varies, king of infinite space,
still bounded by that nutshell, dreaming badly,
unfree to cease to be.

But we – we feel ourselves of different stock,
performing once (or, better, improvising)
a life unauthored, a story yet unlived.
I could, for instance, turn off the computer
and carve a bloody scrawl across my wrists
using, say, a bare steak-knife from the drainer.
I won't (this poem still needs revision) – but
the point is that no Shakespeare sounds *my* stops . . . .
Do you believe this? Do you feel so free?
Nor I. In fact, the chance of slaughtering self
is nil in the present scene. A choice? Not so.
This feels determined, deeply, physically,
in every stitch of skin and puff of breath.
So being is free, but not non-being?

Or neither one. The Player sheds his tears,
but in a fiction, in a dream of passion,
the Prince compares himself unfavorably
while you and I avoid a certain conclusion:
Being free is –
            [*Curtain*]

ANSWER TO SIMMIAS

> Simmias, if I remember rightly, has fears and misgivings
> whether the soul, being in the form of harmony,
> although a fairer and diviner thing than the body,
> may not perish first.
>
> Plato, Phaedo

This happened to me once: I wrote a chaconne
for orchestra (these were my student days),
I scored the thing, took pains, and heard my phrases
begin to soar above their grounded bass.
And then I lost the pages, God knows how.
Those precious, scribbled staves just disappeared
beneath the waves of senior-year disorder.
I wasn't daunted, though. I could still hear it,
the music in my "head," my "thoughts," my "mind":
unscientific terms: had I dropped dead
that day, the probing scalpels would have failed
to find a single quaver in my brain.
Yet they were there, I heard it, wrote it down
again – improved it, even, took it closer
to what I had in mind.
                        Now please imagine
your soul as music. You live out your years
becoming rhythm, harmony, the structure
of what you are. Then comes the final measure,
the whole-note rest of death. The printed score –
your blood and bones and breath and DNA –
will decompose, will disappear as quickly
as my first-draft chaconne. What of the music?
How can you live again? A greater mind
must needs remember you and let you play
forever, each thematic line perfected
and finally sounding true. Heaven is sounding
impossible these days, with every quantum

of matter mathematically weighed and accounted for.
But it's no more, or less, miraculous
than what I have in mind.
     And so, *da capo:*
the choirmaster smiles and gives the downbeat,
the angels pluck you out upon their lyres
while voices far more absolute, more lovely
than any you imagined sing the burden,
as light as life. Simmias, let us pray:
Remember us, O Lord. Keep us in mind.

YOUR MOODS ARE ORCHESTRAL, BUT

don't try to be ironic with the trombones.
That's a cliché, sliding down like that,
not even Béla Bartók could be ironic
with trombones. And the skirling piccolo
is overused, it draws attention
to itself, you sacrifice coherence
for brilliance. Shostakovich himself
did poorly with the piccolo,

Now the full rich strings, that's a different
story, here your orchestration blooms
like a wet gardenia in June, and bursts.
Beautiful, beautiful, beautiful, fortissimo,
subito pianissimo,
such mellifluous control
your conductor wields over
the dynamics of her tyrannized fiddlers,

but why the snare drum, why the cheap celeste-
effect just now? I smell satire
and you know how I hate satire.
Furthermore, I'm dying
for a little counterpoint. Color
as sensuous as Ravel's is all very well
but without form what
is the point?

French horns kiss me smack
in the middle of the recapitulation
and even not knowing
the score I kiss back.

THE SEARCH ENGINE MEDITATES ON "GUATEMALA" AND "POETRY"

Poetry is omnipresent,
vigorous and
enhances **Guatemalan** ...

In the village of Ciudad Vieja,
just outside **Guatemala**'s capital,
.... **Poetry** Slam in Zimbabwe:

Testimony of
death-squad threats ... **Guatemala**
leaves no proof, and immigration judges are suspicious ...

I was living
in **Guatemala** at that time; it was there
that I learned ...

During the 1970s
and 1980s there was
a flourishing of women's **poetry**
in **Guatemala**, much of it
from a feminist, political perspective that was
mostly from a ...

("Living Without **Guatemala**"). If
men disappear into the foliage hiding from ...

It is
nonsense
to talk
about **poetry**, as
most poets
and critics today ...

our century
continues
on its merry way
with the horrors
of **Guatemala**, Tibet, ...

(**Guatemala, Guatemala Guatemala**) –
This thin book
acquaints readers to well-known
poetry over a range of ...
See all my reviews.

But the 'Silent Holocaust' of **Guatemala** was
extraordinarily brutal even by the ... Beautiful
moving and hart-
wrenching **poetry**... a brave, bold and important ...

Fiction, **Poetry**,
non-fiction, and art, Thirty-five
years ... They could not use
the **Guatemalan** postal service because
the man whose ...

Although LGTB organizations have
emerged in **Guatemala**,
hate crimes ... this group were very discreet,
consisting mostly of reading and discussing **poetry**. ...

Spanish language
schools
in **Guatemala**
(Latin America) .... **Poetry**
often has
such qualities. But

to make sure that
your reader understands
and appreciates ...

Roxana from **Guatemala**.
Comment 41 of 47,
added on April 12th, 2007 at 6:09 PM.
... The **poetry** forum
is the
proper place for
questions. ...

ELVIS IN NARNIA

There he is, in his sequined jumpsuit,
manning the prow of the *Dawn Treader*.

Later, "Don't be cruel," he murmurs into the mic
and does that thing with his hips, to the elves.

The four English children stare and point:
"I think it's a sort of satyr, perhaps?"
"No, those are boots, not hooves, I think."

He shows up at Cair Paravel, strides into the throne room.
Modestly: "Anythin I cn do t help, mam?"
Caspian, gently: "I am a prince, good fellow."
"I do pologize, yr majesty. It's the long hair."

Wise and courteous, he doesn't mention that he is
a king in his own country.

With his entourage of beavers and giants and what-all
taking care of business, he's booked across the realm.
He sings the early Sun Records stuff
for the talking animals, who totally get it.
The Vegas period goes over big at tournaments.
"In the Ghetto" is a hit all over again, Number Four
With an Arrowhead.

The King at sunset, kneeling for Aslan's blessing.
The Lion speaks: "You must return to your own land now."

And soon he is legend, Elvis of Memphis,
troubadour from that fallen world
where God took human form.

THE GRAVE-DIGGER'S SONG

> [*Throws up another skull*]
> – stage direction, *Hamlet*, Act V, Scene 1

Yorick is dead, he's all chap-fallen –
someone must take his place.
Hamlet, revenge! your fate is a-callin',
constricting infinite space
to a 'stachio shell.
    Hey ho, ready or no –
    Throw up another skull!

Ophelia's loose in the lobby – let's look!
This isn't the groaning she's wishing for,
while daddy Polonius can't set the hook
in that carp of truth he's been fishing for,
tedious old fool!
    Hey ho, he's first to go –
    Throw up another skull!

Rosie and Goldie arrive for a visit,
the Prince is in fine, antic fettle.
"Welcome, dear friends!" "My lord, what is it
that troubles you?" England will settle
the hash of these gulls.
    Hey ho, reap what you sow –
    Throw up two more skulls!

Opening night for "The Mouse-trap": the plot
has been baited to capture a rat.
Gonzago is poisoned – the King likes it not –
our playwright, marking that,
takes a curtain call.
    Hey ho, let's put on a show! –
    Throw up another skull!

Now riddle me this: A son spares his mother,
a nephew his uncle at prayer;
an eavesdropper drops in the place of another,
his daughter the water won't spare –
can you follow the falls?
    Hey ho, so many laid low –
    Throw up two more skulls!

Brother Laertes is baying for blood
since his family's abrupt diminution.
Cut Hamlet's throat? Yes, that would be good,
but the King has a better solution:
a bogus duel.
    Hey ho, he'll never know –
    Throw up another skull!

A palpable hit! The Prince can fence!
Laertes is starting to ruffle.
He blindsides the Prince, the Prince can sense
a set-up, a swindle – so shuffle
that mortal foil!
    Hey ho, it's blow for blow –
    Throw up two more skulls!

Tragical, comical, sad and absurd,
and soon the whole lot are a-dyin'.
Some lout from Norway gets the last word –
Denmark's a grave to lie in –
the rest is silence.
    Hey ho, *must* you go? –
    Throw up another, yes and another,
    throw up another, another, another,
    throw up a Globe of skulls!

THE COLLECTION REVIEWED
                 – Hirshhorn Museum, Aug. 24

Outside, rain bombarding my umbrella,
I bought a Tootsie Roll from the lone vendor,
a wet Vietnamese in a plastic poncho
huddled beneath her awning. "Bad for business."
The Mall deserted. "*Terrible* for business."

The museum itself contained intriguing people,
dry, and half of them were women. I drifted
aloofly through the galleries, reviewing
the collection. Comfy paired armchairs circled
a central hub so we could rest and stare at

rain exploding in the puddled courtyard.
A sullen youngster, bare heels up on the chair-edge,
used her knees as an escritoire to scribble
a postcard. Imagine if I were lurking near her
to *interact* with her! In a foreign accent:

"To whom are you writing? Please? I am only . . . curious."
Modigliani metal people, diminutive Matisses.
Two gigantic installations, each a challenge:
Where is art? What are borders?
A stack of sheets: Paper. Please take one.

The video of a plain person sucking
her big toe provoked a mild sexual
suspense in me. The dénouement was modern,
though: she took the toe from her mouth and looked at it.
And then put it back in again, pensively,

as the tape looped. Two sweat-suited students
and then a third entered and stood beside me.

The guard – short hair, nightstick – came in. "I love it,
watching people look at that thang." Chuckles.
I remained aloof. "Yall's reactions

are a helluvalot more interesting than *her toe*."
"Is that the uh? the artist? sucking the toe there?"
"Uh huh." "Does she live around here?" "Don't believe so."
The third, not to the guard, sotto voce:
"She a lesbian?" "*Shhh!*" The guard was a woman,

so were the two in sweat suits. Dear confusion!
Heartened, leaving, I saw a sunbeam brighten
a floor installed with silver-wrapped candy:
Please take one, but please refrain from eating
until you are outside the museum.
                                      Thank you.

ONLY PASSING THROUGH

Books were tough bones, once,
they kept you upright, gave you something
strong beneath your easily insulted flesh.
You finished a good book
and it was yours, part of the skeleton, the articulation
of self – you could feel it when you pressed
hard.

And a lifetime of years and words go by and
now books refresh you, they cleanse and cool –
they're like sprinklers you ran through
as a child on a summer morning, reflecting
whatever light is already there. The brief *ahah!* Nothing
you'd ever keep, or want to.
You forget them as soon as they're read.
Who can remember every sun-shower?
"Yes," you say of a recent book,
"I think I read that, last year. I recall
liking it. It was good,
wasn't it?" And it's becoming true
of music too, and places,
and thoughts. The gleaming lawn,
the mirrored light, and you, only passing through.

About the Author

J. Morris has published fiction and poetry in more than 90 literary magazines in the U.S. and Great Britain, including *The Southern Review, Missouri Review, Five Points, Prairie Schooner, Subtropics, Fulcrum,* and *Poetry East*. A first-prize winner in the 2002 Big City Lit poetry contest, his work has been nominated for a Pushcart Prize and reprinted in *Twentieth Century Literary Criticism* and *Anatomy of a Short Story* (Continuum Press). His chapbook, *The Musician, Approaching Sleep*, appeared in 2006 from Dos Madres Press. A short story collection, *When I Snap My Fingers You Will Remember Everything,* was published by No Record Press in 2016. His musical project, Mulberry Coach, a collaboration with singer and lyricist Katie Fisher, released its seventh CD in 2017.

Author photo by Glen Yakushiji

Other books by J. Morris
published by Dos Madres Press

The Musician, Approaching Sleep (2006)

He is also included in:
Realms of the Mothers:
The First Decade of Dos Madres Press (2016)

For the full Dos Madres Press catalog:
www.dosmadres.com